TEE TIME ON THE MOON

HOW ASTRONAUT ALAN SHEPARD PLAYED LUNAR GOLF

DAVID A. KELLY   Illustrated by EDWIN FOTHERINGHAM

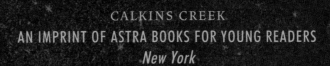

CALKINS CREEK

AN IMPRINT OF ASTRA BOOKS FOR YOUNG READERS
New York

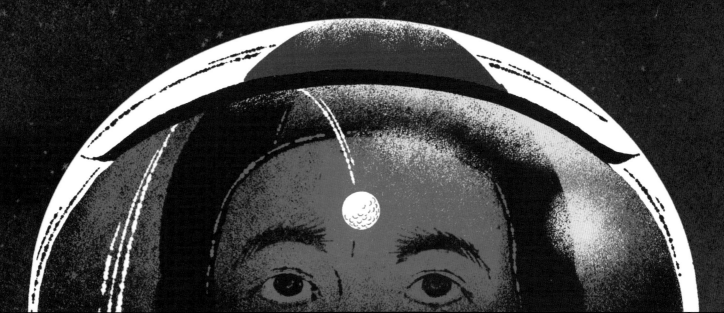

Alan Shepard Jr. had a secret. A secret he was taking to the Moon.

Shepard's fellow astronauts, Stuart Roosa and Edgar Mitchell, were not in on his secret. They didn't know that Shepard had brought something special with him—in a sock.

It was 1971 and the Apollo 14 mission would land humans on the Moon for the third time. Apollo 11 and Apollo 12 had proved that Moon landings were possible, but the Apollo 14 astronauts planned to explore more ground and gather more rock samples.

The astronauts rode to the Moon in the command module of the Apollo spacecraft. Two of them would descend to the Moon in a different part of the spacecraft, called the lunar module.

SATURN V

USA

Commander Shepard waited for the engines of his Saturn V rocket to ignite in a rush of fire and hot gas that would propel Apollo 14 from Florida to the Moon.

LIFTOFF!

Three days later, Shepard and Mitchell entered the lunar module. Roosa would remain behind in the command module and circle the Moon over thirty times, waiting for his partners to return.

The lunar module descended to the Moon and landed.
Shepard and Mitchell quickly got to work.
Shepard's secret would have to wait.

Shepard and Mitchell pulled on their space suits. They were bulky and stiff, making it hard to bend or move, but the astronauts needed them to stay alive. The layers of fabric and insulation in the space suits guarded against radiation and extreme temperatures. A large backpack provided oxygen to breathe and cooling so the astronauts wouldn't overheat. If the space suits failed, the astronauts would die.

There was no time to waste. Shepard and Mitchell set up a television camera so people on Earth could watch them explore the Moon. They deployed instruments to measure moonquakes, lunar dust, and more. They hiked six hundred feet away from the landing site to collect soil and rock samples to take back to Earth.

Then they returned to the spacecraft to rest and sleep.

The next day, Shepard and Mitchell hiked more than a mile and a half while dragging a little trailer to collect rock samples. The trailer let them go farther than any other lunar exploration. But along the way, they encountered rough terrain with large boulders and had to carry the trailer for part of the time.

Despite the challenges, Shepard and Mitchell completed their scientific goals. They collected more than 93 pounds of lunar rocks and soil for research. These rocks had come from Moon volcanoes that had erupted over four billion years ago. Scientists would now know more about how the solar system was formed.

After loading the rock samples into the lunar module, Alan Shepard knew it was time to share his secret with the world.

NASA engineers and a golf pro back on Earth had helped Shepard find a way to attach a golf club head to the handle of an aluminum rock scoop. From one of the pockets in his space suit, he pulled out the metal head and two golf balls!

Shepard snapped the head onto the scoop handle to create
a makeshift MOON CLUB!
Alan Shepard planned to play golf on the Moon.

Playing golf wasn't one of the official experiments.
But Shepard loved golf, and he wanted to see how far a
golf ball would travel on the Moon. With virtually no
atmosphere, and with gravity that is only one-sixth of Earth's,
a golf ball hit on the Moon should travel a LOT farther
than it would on Earth. . . .

But exactly how far?

In front of the television camera and with millions of people watching, Shepard dropped the first golf ball onto the lunar dust.

The space suit made it hard to swing. And the helmet made it hard to look down. But Shepard would take his best shot.

He grabbed his homemade Moon club
with his thick astronaut gloves and . . .

SWUNG

The ball barely moved.

Shepard's first swing had just nudged the ball. The bulky space suit and helmet made it difficult for Shepard to aim the club correctly.

He took a second swing.

The Moon club hit the lunar dust, completely missing the ball!

Shepard teed up again.

He took a third swing.

It connected—but not very well.

The ball bobbled into a nearby crater.

So far, it wasn't a good day on the golf course!

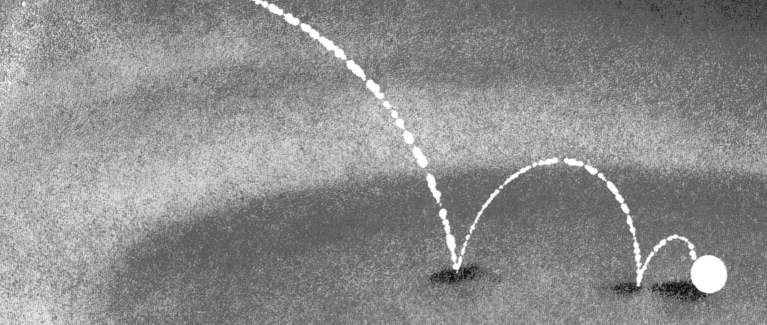

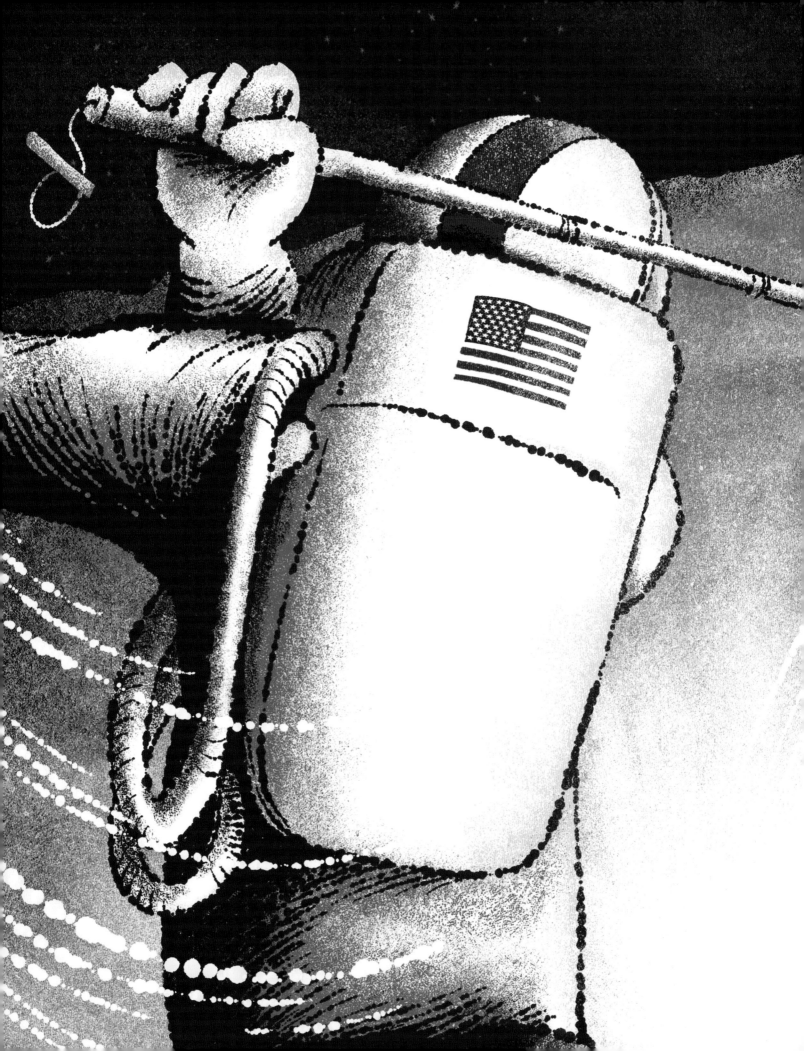

Shepard had one more chance.

He took out his second and last golf ball and dropped it on the lunar soil.

Shepard studied the shot. He swung his club the best he could.

POW!

The golf ball flew into the lunar distance. On Earth, air resistance and gravity would limit how far it could travel. But on the Moon, the ball soared in the Moon's low gravity and minimal atmosphere. It disappeared from television screens and landed somewhere in the distance.

How far did the golf ball go?

"Miles and miles and miles!" Shepard said to everyone watching on Earth.

But no one knew for sure.

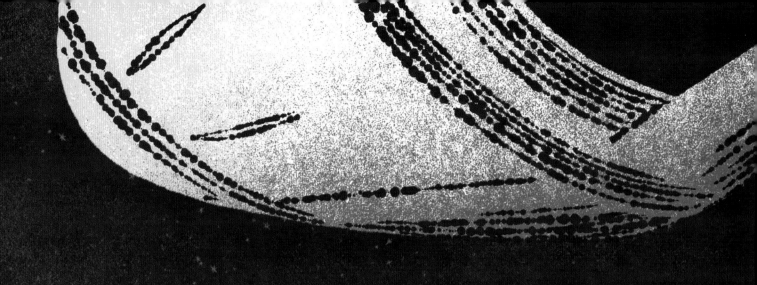

Shepard and Mitchell crawled inside the lunar module and blasted off to meet up with Roosa.

Three days later, the astronauts splashed down in the Pacific Ocean with 93 pounds of Moon rocks—and no golf balls.

The Apollo 14 mission was a huge success. It proved that astronauts could successfully cover long distances on foot and travel far away from their lander. The rocks they brought back helped scientists learn new things about the solar system. And the scientific experiments the mission left on the Moon helped people understand the Moon's geology better.

But one mystery remained.

How far did Alan Shepard's golf ball actually fly?

Almost fifty years later, British photographer Andy Saunders used software to sharpen up old Apollo 14 pictures. He could see the landing site and the abandoned television camera. He even saw Shepard's footprints clearly in the dust. And when he looked into the distance, he spotted two white golf balls!

Saunders calculated the position of the golf balls and precisely how far they had flown.

Did Shepard's second golf ball *really* travel for miles and miles? Not even close. Only *120 feet*!

Although his long-distance drive flew about the length of a few school buses, Alan Shepard scored an out-of-this-world feat—becoming the first human to play a sport on the Moon.

Alan Shepard's Moon golf shots encouraged television
viewers around the world to think differently about the
Moon—as a place they might visit one day.

Experts still believe that a *professional* golfer could hit
a golf ball for miles and miles on the Moon, just like Shepard
said. Andy Saunders calculated that a *good* golfer could hit
a ball over three miles.

It's just that no one has done it.

Yet.

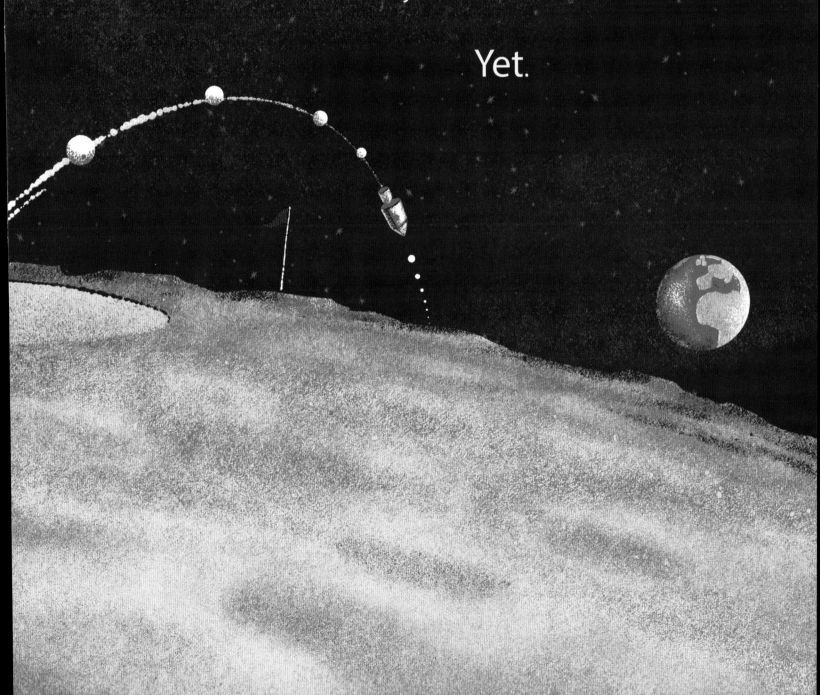

Apollo 14 crew: Alan B. Shepard Jr., Stuart A. Roosa, Edgar D. Mitchell

The Apollo missions to the Moon took place between 1968 and 1972. They were named after Apollo, the Greek god of light, music, and reason. The missions were designed to put Americans on the Moon and return them safely to Earth. The Apollo program enabled twelve men to walk on the Moon.

The Apollo missions to the Moon used the largest rocket ever built at the time, the Saturn V. It was just about the height of a 36-story building. The Saturn V was composed of three stages (or sections). Each stage would fall away to Earth or crash into the moon once its fuel was used up. Then the engines of the next stage would fire and push the rest of the rocket (along with the astronauts) into space.

Each Apollo flight to the Moon included three astronauts. When the rocket reached the Moon, the lunar module would separate from the command module. One astronaut would stay behind in the command module as it circled the Moon. The other two astronauts would go down to the Moon in the lunar module. They would remain there for up to three days. Then the two astronauts would blast off from the Moon and catch back up with the command module as it orbited the Moon. The astronauts would then jettison the lunar module and it would crash into the Moon or head off into space. The astronauts would fly back to Earth together in the command module and splashdown in the ocean, where a US Navy ship picked them up.

A big goal of the Apollo missions was to learn more about the Moon and solar system. They did that by taking pictures of the Moon and Earth, conducting experiments on the way to the Moon and back, collecting soil and rock samples from the Moon, and leaving experiments behind on the Moon after they left.

The Apollo missions that went to the Moon were:

Apollo 8—(December 21–27, 1968) Crew: Frank Borman, William A. Anders, James A. Lovell Jr.

Apollo 8 was the first human mission to fly to the Moon. It took just under three days to get there. The astronauts orbited the Moon ten times, taking pictures of possible landing sites for future missions. They also made a famous Christmas Eve television broadcast to wish a Merry Christmas and send a blessing to everyone on Earth.

Selected accomplishments: Apollo 8 was the first crewed mission to travel to the Moon. It was also the first to see and take a picture of an "earthrise," or the point in an orbit of the Moon when the Earth rises above the surface, just as the Moon does on Earth.

Apollo 9—(March 3–13, 1969) Crew: James McDivitt, David R. Scott, Russell Schweickart.

Apollo 9, did not travel to the Moon. Instead, it traveled into Earth's orbit and tested out the lunar module.

Apollo 10—(May 18–26, 1969) Crew: Thomas Stafford, Eugene A. Cernan, John Young

Apollo 10 was a dress rehearsal for the first Moon landing. Apollo 10 flew to the Moon and tested the lunar module. Astronauts Stafford and Cernan flew it down to about 50,000 feet above the Moon's surface, but they did not land.

Selected accomplishments: Apollo 10 proved that the lunar module could descend to the Moon and dock back up with the command module. It also gathered important data on gravitational effects, and checked out flight control systems, television transmissions, and many other tracking and guidance systems.

Apollo 11—(July 16–24, 1969) Crew: Neil Armstrong, Edwin E. "Buzz" Aldrin Jr., Michael Collins

Apollo 11 was the first mission to land humans on the Moon. Neil Armstrong became the first person to set foot on the Moon, and Buzz Aldrin followed. Armstrong and Aldrin planted an American flag, took pictures, and collected lunar rock and soil samples during their stay.

Selected accomplishments: Apollo 11 achieved the primary mission of taking humans to the Moon and returning them safely. It also transmitted television signals from the Moon so people around the world could watch the astronauts explore the Moon. In addition, Apollo 11 deployed several scientific experiments, including ones that gathered information on solar wind and the seismic activity of the Moon. The astronauts gathered Moon rocks and soil for analysis and deployed a laser ranging retroreflector (LRRR) for measuring the exact distance between the Earth and the Moon.

Apollo 12—(November 14–24, 1969) Crew: Charles Conrad Jr., Alan L. Bean, Richard F. Gordon Jr.

Apollo 12 was struck by a giant lightning bolt just as it was taking off. A massive surge of electricity ran from the top of the rocket to the bottom. But Apollo 12 took off safely and made it to the Moon. Its astronauts took two moonwalks and brought back pieces of an earlier, uncrewed spacecraft to study. NASA had sent the spacecraft to see if the moon was solid enough to support an Apollo lunar module (it was!).

Selected accomplishments: Apollo 12 studied landing sites for future Moon missions, developed techniques for more precise landings, and undertook extended periods of working on the Moon. After reuniting in orbit above the Moon, the astronauts disconnected from the lunar module. They then directed it to crash into the Moon so the resulting seismic shock could be measured.

Apollo 13—(April 11–17, 1970) Crew: James A. Lovell Jr., Fred W. Haise Jr., John L. "Jack" Swigert Jr.

Apollo 13 didn't land men on the Moon because the mission had a severe malfunction on its way there. Conditions grew so bad that it was possible that the astronauts could have died. Instead, on-the-fly assistance from NASA engineers helped figure out ways to patch the damage and get the men back home. Apollo 13 ended up circling the Moon and flying safely back to Earth.

Selected accomplishments: Apollo 13 didn't achieve its original objectives but was considered a success because the mission safely returned its three-person crew to Earth. The mission also highlighted the ability of the flight controllers on the ground to quickly come up with novel solutions to unexpected problems.

Apollo 14—(January 31–February 9, 1971) Crew: Alan B. Shepard Jr., Edgar D. Mitchell, Stuart A. Roosa

Featured in this book, Shepard and Mitchell completed two moonwalks. Shepard traveled more than 9,000 feet on the Moon, a new record. In addition, it was the first time that two sports were played on the Moon. Shepard played golf with his two golf balls, and Mitchell threw an improvised javelin made from a metal rod.

Alan Shepard plants the American flag on the Moon.

Selected accomplishments: Apollo 14 was the first mission to use a wheeled transport vehicle on the Moon. It also made the most precise landing to date. In addition, the mission brought back more lunar samples than any previous mission, and its astronauts had the longest moonwalk time to date and covered the most lunar distance (over two miles). The mission also deployed a solar wind experiment and a multipurpose set of experiments called the Apollo Lunar Surface Experiments Package (ALSEP).

Apollo 15—(July 26–August 7, 1971) Crew: David R. Scott, James B. Irwin, Alfred M. Worden

Apollo 15 featured an upgraded lunar module that could stay on the Moon longer, bring more experiments, and support greater surface mobility for the astronauts. The Apollo 15 astronauts used the first Lunar Roving Vehicle (LRV), a car for the Moon.

Selected accomplishments: The Apollo 15 mission evaluated the new, upgraded Apollo equipment, explored the Hadley-Apennine region where it landed, and set up scientific experiments on the lunar surface. Scott and Irwin spent more than eighteen hours exploring the Moon's surface and traveled over seventeen miles in their lunar rover. The crew also evaluated upgraded space suits and deployed a small satellite while orbiting the Moon that would be used to study the Moon's gravitational variations.

Apollo 16—(April 16–27, 1972) Crew: John W. Young, Charles M. Duke Jr., Thomas K. Mattingly II

The Apollo 16 crew used a lunar rover and got it up to just over 10 miles per hour! They spent just under three days on the Moon's surface and conducted three moonwalks. They also picked up the largest Moon rock ever returned to Earth, Big Muley. The rock was named after Bill Muehlberger, the Apollo 16 field geology team leader.

Selected accomplishments: Apollo 16 inspected, surveyed, and sampled the lunar surface at its landing site in the Descartes region of the Moon. It also deployed experiments on the Moon's surface, as previous missions had done. The Apollo 16 astronauts pushed the lunar rover to the limit by driving it through tight turns and short stops.

Apollo 17—(December 7–19, 1972) Crew: Eugene A. Cernan, Harrison H. Schmitt, Ronald E. Evans

In 1972, Apollo 17 ended up being the last Apollo mission to the Moon. After Apollo 11 had successfully landed Americans on the Moon in 1969, there was less public support for the tremendously expensive and risky Apollo program. Americans of the 1970s were more concerned about the Vietnam War, poverty, problems in cities, and environmental crises than they were about continuing missions to the Moon. When this book was written in 2022, no one had walked on the Moon since the Apollo astronauts. Hopefully, that will change soon!

Selected accomplishments: Apollo 17 explored a region of the Moon that contained both older and younger rocks than any of the previous missions. Apollo 17 astronaut Harrison Schmitt was the only professional geologist to land on and explore the Moon. The crew completed three moonwalks and spent the longest time outside the lunar module (more than 22 hours) and traveled farther from it (over four miles) than any other crew. They returned with just over 243 pounds of lunar samples!

COMMANDER ALAN SHEPARD

Shepard was the second person and first American in space. On May 5, 1961, he rode his Freedom 7 space capsule to an altitude of more than 116 miles above the Earth. But his early success was sidelined by Ménière's disease, a condition in which fluid pressure builds up in the inner ear. Once his disease was discovered, he was grounded from flying into space again and named Chief of the Astronaut Office, where he managed the

astronaut corp. Six years later, he had surgery to correct the problem and was cleared to fly into space again in 1969. He was initially assigned to fly Apollo 13, but Shepard and his crew were switched to Apollo 14. At age 47, Shepard was the oldest astronaut to walk on the Moon.

Strange Experiments on Apollo 14

The astronauts on Apollo 14 did some unusual things. Commander Alan Shepard Jr. played golf on the Moon. Stuart Roosa brought along hundreds of tree seeds in a canister that orbited the Moon with him. They were subsequently planted throughout the United States and known as "Moon trees." And Edgar Mitchell secretly brought along 25 numbered cards to try ESP (extrasensory perception) experiments with collaborators on Earth during his rest periods.

What Happened to the Moon Club?

Shepard's original moon club is on display at the United States Golf Association (USGA) Museum in Liberty Corner, New Jersey. The golf club head was a Wilson Staff Dyna-Power 6-iron head.

A Moon Experiment That's Still Shining

Laser distance experiments left behind over 50 years ago by Apollo missions 11, 14, and 15 are still being used for scientific research today! The laser ranging retroreflector (LRRR) experiment was a small platform filled with quartz-glass prisms that reflect light. Scientists use telescopes on Earth to aim laser beams at the reflectors. They measure the time it takes for the pulse of laser light to return to Earth from the Moon. The results enable scientists to calculate the exact distance between the Earth and the Moon, to a fraction of an inch. Even though the Moon is an average of 239,000 miles away, this experiment has shown that the distance between the Earth and the Moon has been growing by 1.5 inches per year.

Treasures from History

Sometimes it's good to hold on to things, like treasures from the Moon and artifacts from the Apollo missions. Over time, technology advances and allows researchers to learn new things from old items. For example, most of the Moon rocks brought back to Earth by the Apollo missions were soon distributed to researchers around the world for study. While the rocks were lent out for research, they remained property of the United States government. Some were sealed away untouched, to be examined years later with more advanced technologies. In 2019, nearly fifty years after the last rock was collected from the Moon, NASA distributed these preserved Moon rocks to nine different research teams for ongoing study. In fact, these old Moon rocks are still helping scientists to learn new things about the Moon. For example, a 2021 study by researchers at the University of Hawaii at Mānoa of a Moon rock brought back by Apollo 17 in 1972 showed that after its

formation, the Moon cooled off much faster than previously thought.

Another way new approaches can be used on old treasures is featured in this book, in the way that Andy Saunders used advanced image processing capabilities to pull new information from videos and photographs that were taken during the Moon missions.

Why Moon Golf Mattered

While not entirely scientific, one of the big impacts of Shepard's playing golf on the Moon was to make people think about the differences between the Earth and Moon in terms of gravity and atmosphere. Director Bob Gilruth of NASA's Manned Spacecraft Center was resistant to Shepard's plan for playing golf on the Moon at first. But he eventually relented when he realized it wouldn't impact the mission, and it might engage TV viewers in ways that the collection of Moon rocks couldn't.

Locations of Alan Shepard's golf game on the Moon.

SELECTED BIBLIOGRAPHY

BOOKS

Benson, Charles D., and William B. Faherty. *Moon Launch! A History of the Saturn-Apollo Launch Operations.* Gainesville: University Press of Florida, 2001.

Chaikin, Andrew. *A Man on the Moon: The Voyages of the Apollo Astronauts.* New York: Penguin Books, 1994.

Godwin, Robert, ed. *Apollo 14: The NASA Mission Reports.* Burlington, Canada: Apogee Books, 2001.

———. *Project Apollo: Exploring the Moon.* Burlington, Canada: Apogee Books, 2006.

Mitchell, Edgar, and Ellen Mahoney. *Earthrise: My Adventures as an Apollo 14 Astronaut.* Chicago: Chicago Review Press, 2014.

Murray, Charles, and Catherine Bly Cox. *Apollo: The Race to the Moon.* Burkittsville, MD: South Mountain Books, 2004.

Shepard, Alan, and Deke Slayton. *Moon Shot: The Inside Story of America's Race to the Moon.* Atlanta: Turner Publishing, 1994.

Thompson, Neal. *Light This Candle: The Life & Times of Alan Shepard.* New York: Crown, 2007.

INTERVIEWS

Saunders, Andy. Email correspondence with the author, 2022.

Email interview by the author, January 2022.

ARTICLES*

Catlin, Roger. "When Astronaut Alan Shepard Hit the Golf Shot Heard 'Round the World." *Smithsonianmag.com*, February 3, 2021.

Culpepper, JuliaKate E. "Astronaut Alan Shepard and the 50th Anniversary of the First Golf Swing on the Moon." *USA Today*, February 2, 2021.

Dunbar, Brian. "Apollo 14." NASA. July 8, 2009. nasa.gov/mission_pages/apollo/missions/apollo14.html.

———. "Who Was Alan Shepard?" NASA. June 9, 2015. nasa.gov/audience/forstudents/5-8/features/nasa-knows/who-was-alan-shepard-58.html.

"Earth's Moon." NASA. August 9, 2021. solarsystem.nasa.gov/moons/earths-moon/overview.

Ferguson, Doug. "Out of This World: Shepard Put Golf on Moon 50 Years Ago." Phys.org. February 5, 2021. phys.org/news/2021-02-world-shepard-golf-moon-years.html.

"In Depth." NASA. April 9, 2019. solarsystem.nasa.gov/missions/apollo-14/in-depth.

"Lunar and Planetary Institute." *Apollo 14 Mission Overview*, Lunar and Planetary Institute. lpi.usra.edu/lunar/missions/apollo/apollo_14.

Mars, Kelli. "50 Years Ago: Apollo 14 Heads for Home." NASA. nasa.gov/feature/50-years-ago-apollo-14-heads-for-home.

———. "50 Years Ago: Apollo 14 Lands at Fra Mauro." NASA. February 4, 2021. nasa.gov/feature/50-years-ago-apollo-14-lands-at-fra-mauro.

———. "50 Years Ago: Apollo 14 Launches to the Moon." NASA. February 1, 2021. nasa.gov/feature/50-years-ago-apollo-14-launches-to-the-moon.

Saunders, Andy. "The Mystery Behind Alan Shepard's 'Moon Shot' Revealed." USGA. February 5, 2021. usga.org/content/usga/home-page/articles/2021/02/shepard-moon-club-50th-anniversary-usga-museum.html#returnable.

Trostel, Michael. "3 Things: The Moon Club." *US Golfing Association*. April 3, 2019. usga.org/content/usga/home-page/articles/2019/02/three-things-alan-shepard-moon-club.html.

*Websites active at time of publication

MORE TO EXPLORE

Official Apollo 14 NASA mission webpage. nasa.gov/mission_pages/apollo/apollo-14

To all the space travelers of the future . . . reach for the stars (and Moon)! —*DAK*
For my family, always —*EF*

ACKNOWLEDGMENTS

I am very grateful to Andy Saunders for his helpful feedback, expert Apollo knowledge, and inspiration for this book. Many thanks also to Dr. Jennifer Ross-Nazzal, historian at NASA's Johnson Space Center, for providing her expertise and insights on the Apollo program and Teasel Muir-Harmony, curator of the Apollo Collection at the Smithsonian National Air and Space Museum. Much appreciation to my agent, Caryn Wiseman, and of course, my terrific editor, Carolyn Yoder, who saved me from shanking the story and kept the book on par. And as always, thanks to my first and best reader, my wife, Alice Lesch Kelly.

PICTURE CREDITS

NASA: 34, 36; NASA/JSC/ASU/Andy Saunders: 38.

Calkins Creek
An imprint of Astra Books for Young Readers,
a division of Astra Publishing House
astrapublishinghouse.com
Printed in China

ISBN: 978-1-6626-8017-5 (hc)
ISBN: 978-1-6626-8018-2 (eBook)